First Facts™

Our Physical World

Gravity

by Ellen Sturm Niz

Consultant:
Philip W. Hammer, PhD
Vice President, The Franklin Center
The Franklin Institute
Philadelphia, Pennsylvania

Capstone
press
Mankato, Minnesota

First Facts is published by Capstone Press,
151 Good Counsel Drive, P.O. Box 669, Mankato, Minnesota 56002.
www.capstonepress.com

Library of Congress Cataloging-in-Publication Data
Niz, Ellen Sturm.
    Gravity / by Ellen Sturm Niz; consultant, Philip W. Hammer.
    p. cm.—(First facts. Our physical world)
    Includes bibliographical references and index.
    ISBN–13: 978-0-7368-5403-0 (hardcover)
    ISBN–10: 0-7368-5403-7 (hardcover)
    1. Gravity—Experiments—Juvenile literature. I. Title. II. Series.
QB334.N59 2006
531'.14'078—dc22   2005013324

Summary: Introduces young readers to gravity, its characteristics, and its uses in the world.
    Includes instructions for an activity to demonstrate some of gravity's characteristics.

Editorial Credits
Aaron Sautter, editor; Linda Clavel, set designer; Bobbi J. Dey, book designer;
    Juliette Peters, illustrator; Kelly Garvin, photo researcher/photo editor

Photo Credits
Capstone Press/Karon Dubke, cover, 5, 15, 21
Corbis/G. Kalt, 16; LWA-Dann Tardif, 7; Tom & Dee Ann McCarthy, 18–19
Getty Images Inc./Hulton Archive, 11; Stephen Simpson, 20
NASA/JSC, 12
Peter Arnold, Inc./Astrofoto, 8
Photodisc, 6

1 2 3 4 5 6 11 10 09 08 07 06

Table of Contents

Gravity

Look around the room. Every object you see is pulling on all the other objects with the force of **gravity**. They are even pulling on you!

But the objects don't move. You don't feel them pulling on you. The objects' **masses** are too small. What's big enough to hold your feet on the ground? It's the earth itself!

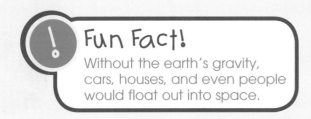

Fun Fact!
Without the earth's gravity, cars, houses, and even people would float out into space.

Earth's Gravity

Earth has a huge mass. Huge objects, like planets, have strong forces of gravity. Smaller objects like people, cars, or even moons, are pulled toward the center of these huge objects.

Everything on earth is pulled toward the planet's center. When you jump into a lake, earth's gravity pulls you down into the water.

Gravity in Space

The moon circles the earth because of gravity. Without the earth's gravity pulling on it, the moon would float away into space.

 Fun Fact!
The moon also pulls on the earth. The moon's gravity pulls on the earth's oceans to create ocean tides.

Just as the earth pulls on the moon, the sun pulls on earth and all the other planets. The sun is so huge that its gravity keeps them all from floating away into space.

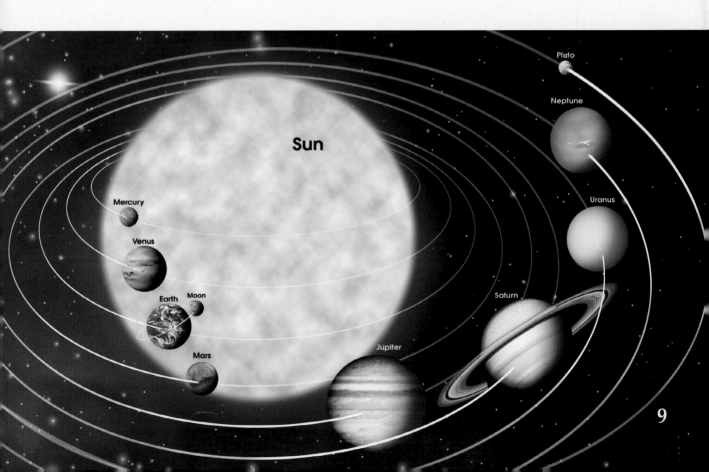

Sir Isaac Newton

Sir Isaac Newton was an English scientist who experimented with gravity. He was the first to discover that the moon circles the earth because of earth's gravity.

Newton learned that the force of gravity works to pull all objects toward each other. Today, his discovery is called the Law of Universal Gravitation.

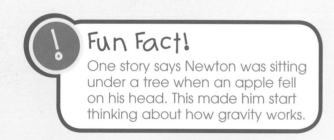

Fun Fact!
One story says Newton was sitting under a tree when an apple fell on his head. This made him start thinking about how gravity works.

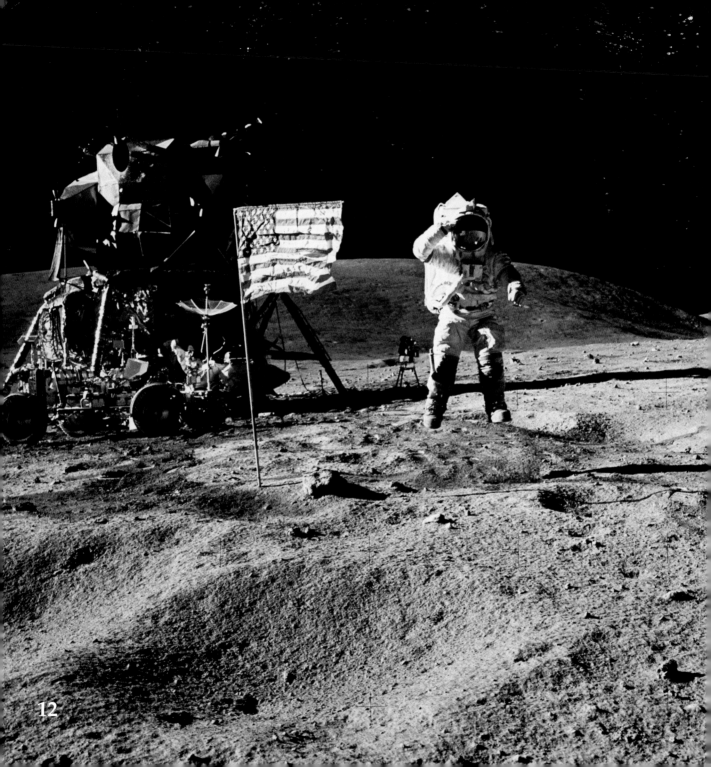

Gravity and Weight

The amount of gravity pulling on a person or object is measured as **weight**. A strong force of gravity makes an object heavy. But a smaller force of gravity makes the same object weigh less.

An astronaut can jump much higher on the moon than on the earth. The moon has a smaller force of gravity than the earth. So everything weighs less there.

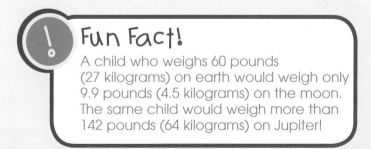

Fun Fact!

A child who weighs 60 pounds (27 kilograms) on earth would weigh only 9.9 pounds (4.5 kilograms) on the moon. The same child would weigh more than 142 pounds (64 kilograms) on Jupiter!

The Pull of Gravity

Try dropping a marble and a big rock from the same height. They will both hit the ground at the same time.

Objects don't fall faster just because they are bigger or heavier. All objects fall at the same speed when gravity is the only force acting on them.

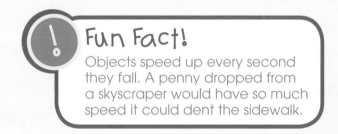

Fun Fact!

Objects speed up every second they fall. A penny dropped from a skyscraper would have so much speed it could dent the sidewalk.

Air Resistance

Air resistance works against the downward pull of gravity. Air pushes up on an object as it falls. An object's shape determines how much air resistance it has.

Air rushes quickly past a skydiver as he falls. There is little air resistance. But the shape of his parachute helps catch the air. This creates more air resistance so the skydiver can slow down and land safely.

Using Gravity

Gravity is useful for work and play. Gravity pulls you toward the ground on a fast slide. Gravity helps water flow from water towers to people's homes. Gravity helps us do many things every day.

Fun Fact!
Nature uses gravity too. Gravity makes rivers flow downhill and helps create waterfalls.

Amazing but True!

Gravity helps us walk straight. Our ears have tiny parts that are filled with fluid. Gravity acts on this fluid to tell us how we move.

Sometimes these parts don't work right. When you spin in a circle and then stop, the fluid in your ears keeps moving. Your brain thinks you are still spinning, so you feel dizzy.

Hands On: Seeing Gravity at Work

Gravity pulls on everything around us. How often do you notice it working? Do the following experiments to see gravity and air resistance at work. Ask an adult to help you with this activity.

What You Need

stepladder   handkerchief
tape measure   safety pin
marble   string
baseball   tape
feather

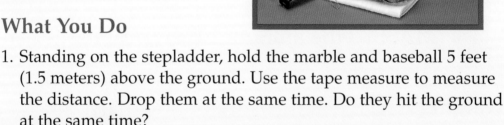

What You Do

1. Standing on the stepladder, hold the marble and baseball 5 feet (1.5 meters) above the ground. Use the tape measure to measure the distance. Drop them at the same time. Do they hit the ground at the same time?
2. Hold the baseball and the feather at the same height as before. Drop them at the same time. Did they hit the ground at the same time?
3. Make a parachute for the marble out of the handkerchief. Pin the four corners of the handkerchief together with the safety pin. Tape the string around the marble and attach it to the safety pin.
4. Now drop the baseball and the marble with the parachute as in Step 1. Do they hit the ground at the same time?

Does an object's weight or mass affect how fast it falls? Does an object's shape affect how fast it falls? Does air resistance affect how fast objects fall?

21

Glossary

air resistance (AIR ri-ZISS-tuhnss)—the force of air that pushes against and slows down moving objects; air pushes up on an object while gravity pulls down.

gravity (GRAV-uh-tee)—a force that pulls objects together; gravity pulls objects toward the center of very large masses, like the earth.

mass (MASS)—the amount of physical matter an object contains

weight (WATE)—a measure of how hard the force of gravity pulls on an object

Read More

Conrad, David. *All Fall Down.* Spyglass Books. Minneapolis, Minn.: Compass Point Books, 2002.

Prasad, Kamal. *Why Can't I Jump Very High? A Book about Gravity.* Santa Rosa, Calif.: Science Square Publishing, 2004.

Trumbauer, Lisa. *What Is Gravity?* Rookie Read-About Science. New York: Children's Press, 2004.

Internet Sites

FactHound offers a safe, fun way to find Internet sites related to this book. All of the sites on FactHound have been researched by our staff.

Here's how:
1. Visit *www.facthound.com*
2. Type in this special code **0736854037** for age-appropriate sites. Or enter a search word related to this book for a more general search.
3. Click on the **Fetch It** button.

FactHound will fetch the best sites for you!

Index